...Just a Season

In no way are my words meant to hurt or show lack of respect for America. I have been a soldier and know all to well the responsibility and oath I took to serve my country. I have no regrets only old wounds, memories and life lessons. My seasons are about me and a time when things were as they were----. I hope that you will see them as such.

J. Monique

Also by J. Monique Gambles

Saturday's Epiphany: Reflections

When The Drama has Ceased

Something About Ginger

Broken Ladder

Ballin' for Natalie

J. Monique Gambles

_____

...Just a Season

A BOLD BOOK

It's BOLD Publishing
Published by It's BOLD Publishing
P.O. BOX 914
Desoto Texas 75123-0914

BOOKS ARE AVAILABLE AT QUANTITY
DISCOUNTS WHEN USED TO PROMOTE
PRODUCTIONS OR SERVICES. FOR INFORMATION
PLEASE WRITE TO MARKETING DIVISION, IT'S
BOLD PUBLISHING P.O. BOX 914 75123-0914

Acknowledgements

Special thanks to my family for your unconditional love and support. No matter what I've aimed to do, you have always encouraged me. Thanks to the far and few, real friends that have been here even when I wasn't. Thanks for holding my hand, wiping away my tears, and understanding who I am. To my Father and his son Jesus Christ, thank you for loving me in spite of my hang-ups and showing me how to love others in spite of theirs.

J. Monique

Foreword

An old friend once told me that there are three reasons why people come into your life; season, reason and a lifetime. I had never heard that and didn't quite understand it until we were no longer friends.

It was just a season, is what I'd often tell myself when I realized why our friendship had to end. I could only laugh at all of the fun times, and cherish the things that helped me to grow. Forever I will look at myself as a work in progress, accepting why they had to go.

Like leaves falling or changing colors and preparing one to reap what you sow, many relationships and situations were just seasons that helped me to grow.

Table of Contents

Women

Family Love

Makemewant2holla

A long walk: war torn Iraq

Interlude…

*Lauren Hill: Unplugged
(both Cd's)*

Part I
Women

Sistah Strut

Strutting her stuff
Broad shoulders, locked & upright,
Seriousness on her face
as she glides with an ass that's tight.
Her eyes searching,
wanting to call someone's bluff
Respectively so, she is Sistah Strut!

A picture of perfect ness
Degreed, achieved, &
a symbol of survival
setbacks, roadblocks & winning
a many of battles.
She has arrived
And amongst many
considered the best
always going for the Gold
and not accepting anything less.

Look at her walk, those shoulders,
Strides and head angled to the sky.
While struggling sistah's
Fall by the wayside
& begin to get high.
Hopeless teenagers are impregnated
with crack babies & deflated dreams
as she looks away willingly,
ignoring their tormented screams.

Gucci down, Prada, or three letters
that may define her.
She struts tight assed glides,

hiding any past reminders.

Don't get me wrong
I don't blame
the possibility of the letters
I blame Sistah Strut
'cause she thinks she's better.

Sistah Strut quit walkin' that walk
& go to local schoolyards,
youth detention centers, jails,
halfway houses & crack spots.
Challenge yourself
by helping someone
else to not give up!
Stop thinking you have to be so high
& competitive with
another sistah strut.
Wake up from that self-inflated ego,
Come on now, I'm callin' Yo Bluff!

Designs of a deep sistah's mind

Not clothes status or woes,
but experience & battle scars
from surviving life's blows.
Her frame is virtuous
& pressure is handled,
and even in a crisis,
she is never dismantled.

It is not her degrees
or what she has achieved
but it is her word
that is DEEP & impeccable
& let us not forget,
that she always
carries herself respectful.

Her tongue cuts one way.
What she say's today
she can say the next day.
She knows to whom she belongs
& as a result, she is strong.
Her weapon is not a knife or deceit
but her knowledge of self
& the spirit of truth that she keeps.

From size two 2 Twenty-two
She's the sistah who's down 4real
and will always be there 4 u.
She doesn't have time to be fake
'cause she knows her soul's at stake.
She's the friend U ought 2 keep
'cause this sistah's real & DEEP.

Stop Sayin' U My Friend

First of all you don't even listen
or understand my shoes
and some battles I must lose.
You don't accept my episodes,
(you know those sporadic loner roads.)

I'm tired of explanin'
or even pretendin'
You see I like being me
and all that I see.
My big lips, small waist,
big feet & big teeth.
Hell, I even like being a 4 or a 6
cause I rarely eat meat!

I know you don't want to see me win
but rather me down
with a face that holds
a pitiful frown
or a hand that has no man
it's my happiness you can't stand
and it is my demise
that you continue to plan.

You don't even know me
my hurt, my strength,
or level of integrity,
and my faith in GOD,
you can't even conceive.
My deliverance you won't accept
nor do you treat me with respect.
Instead you look at me with disdain

9

and utter contempt!

You don't even like me
way down you think I'm some freak.
And with jealous rage,
you pretend and continue
smiling in my face.

Stop sayin' U my friend
'cause this façade has come to an end.

ISSUES

I got issues, U got issues
Everyone's got issues
'cause we all got something
we have to go through.
But I ain't gon' apologize 4 bein' me
or how I have to be.
I love who I am
and I don't need any man
to define, waste time
or F*** with my mind!
Yeah I wear a size 4
and I ain't a whore,
hoe, or bitch!
Hell, I worked for this
with my sweat, tears
and controlling my fears.
Anything I didn't like,
I began to fight,
fought hard, and it was a battle
and with each blow
that came my way
I did my best to handle.
Sistah don't get me wrong
'cause I believe we all can be strong
I understand your fight
and all those sleepless nights.
Sistah I wish I could hold yo' hand
and tell you,
everything's gon' be all right,
and no matter what,
fight, fight, and fight.
But you can't be mad at me

J. Monique Gambles

'cause of who I have to be.

We all have issues
we all have something
that we are going through.

UnknownMother

I saw her over there standing
With a nappy Afro, no front teeth
And nasty clothes that were saggin'
Her skin was a mixture of chocolate
and a swirl of charcoal
She looked at me with vacant eyes
with a devil's smile
and a shadow of her soul.

Not even the wind could move her
Or rain to cause her to wince.
She was like an old abandoned building
still standing after decades spent.

I couldn't take my eyes off her
'cause I saw within her
the strangest resemblance
chills crept across my body
and I was suddenly tense.

That could have been my mother
or better yet, me
I ignored the horns
blowin' in the background
'cause for a moment
I thought she mouthed "please"

I was stuck in time
sad memories filled my mind.
Then I saw red
which in an instant
escalated the budding pain

dancing in my head.

Her eyes poked me on the shoulder
and I looked over once again.
This time I surveyed her entire body
and noticed her stomach covered in Hammy downs
was protruding.

My tears did appear
and I searched frantically
in my purse
but quickly realized I was broke
and had nothing to spare.

She knew it too,
'cause she shot me a sarcastic grin.
I smiled slightly
shrugged my shoulders,
and breathed a hurtful sigh.
She turned aimlessly
and began walkin'
and as the light turned green,
I mouthed back "goodbye"

Pretty Soon

There's no more that I can give
'cause I'm gon' die while you live.
I'm used up and sucked dry.
Beaten down, trodden upon
as you began to rise.

I've given the best of me
and was held captive
while you ran free.
Even pumped you up
and held your hand.
You turned yo' back
to be with "so called friends"
and "any man."

I actually have nothing left
Pretty soon
I'm gon' take my last breath.
I'm empty on the inside
'cause for this friendship,
I've tried and I've tried.

I've taken the back seat,
saw defeat,
had to hide
and heard one too many lies.

In an emotional sense,
I've been an ATM, cash register,
and a platinum credit card
with unlimited withdrawals.
And you, you've been a lone star card

SSI, and a bounced check!

This much I do hate
for what I've given
in this friendship,
you have yet to reciprocate.

Clandenstinestateofmind

It is the opposite of shine
often kept in the back of ones mind.
It can be dressed up fear
or secret thoughts
of wanting someone near.

For me,
It was once a past
that I was ashamed of.
A future unobtainable,
memories unbearable,
and going forward unthinkable.

Until I promised myself before GOD
no longer would I allow clandestine
to be a word used to define,
or something to remind,
me of a tore up state of mind.

It would serve only as a "purpose"
to be a reminder of "forgiveness"
and knowledge that "I can do this"
and only used to "reminisce"

A New Walk

(Success is a journey within the soul)

Leaves fallin' from the trees
Autumns cool breeze.
There are some things
I now see,
like life, the true Israelites
& the rumors of war
as opposed to what I saw.

There is a difference
in my shoes
which make a different sound,
as I now walk, tall & proud.
I see in between the lies
& the schemes
and the fact that things
aren't always as they seem.
Cause I see hatred
unlike before
& the absence of spirituality, replaced with
the presence of the Whore.

I finally see the line
between good & evil
the masquerade in Christianity
(oh yes, I now see through you)
Your rearranged maps
and unexplained mishaps(ENRON)
stolen elections(2000)
an abundance of deception(911)
holding me back
even with a degree

& N-words with money

thinkin' they free. (Black republicans!)
But with knowledge
I do hold the key,
unlocking the chains
of a bewildered society.
I'm here with
the book in my hand
Scripture to scripture
verse to verse
I KNOW WHO I AM.

It's a brand new day
spiritual opposition,
and deception
has been erased!

A true descendent
of Abraham Isaac & Jacob
I understand the plight
of a spiritual man.
The truth in His word
and the fulfillment
of scripture,
the mystery of Babylon,
Africa & Israel the political.

Lover's Quarrel (fighting with GOD)

Love so sweet,
like golden paved streets
Through rain, snow,
sleet we often meet.
An invocation, exaltation
My tribulation & contemplation
Your Love unconditional, awesome
Merciful & filled with dedication

O' but I listened to my girls.
Torn & scorned I ignored the horn
instead I listened to the beat,
which ultimately became my defeat.
My actions became my words
& I got what I deserved.
Confused & ambivalent,
I did not the will of my Master
but another I served.

Adamant & blocked headed
I ignored my path
Until you stopped me,
then rocked me
with your mighty wrath.
I then realized my wrong
& the pain that I caused
but you wiped away my tears
& reminded me, I'm still yours.

My path for you has now truly begun
& we are no longer quarrelsome,
but are ONE.

A Diamond in the rough

As I shake off the matter
that once covered me,
a smile dances across my face
'cause people can finally see
that I have arrived
and survived such hard times
and the sparkles represent
"my time to shine."

But I can remember
So many times
 I didn't want to persevere
'cause time and time again,
I believed life wasn't fair.
Mama was gone by eleven
And Daddy, he was gone way before then.

With my exceptionalities,
I was reminded often
That nothing would be me.
Along with societies blatant attacks
I ignored those notions
and lived based on the facts.

My heritage, ancestry
& a visible mentor's strong will
I lived with hope,
knowing my dreams I would
someday fulfill.
I thank God today
that I didn't give up when life was tough
'cause beneath it all, I was simply

J. Monique Gambles   . . . Just a Season
a Diamond in the rough

Know to whom you belong

Did I tell you,
that I danced with the DEVIL? Yep,
& that brotha
looked right into my eyes.
I was so taken & awestruck
it was as if I was high.
'cause that brotha put me in a trance
& only with him, did I want to dance.

He pretended to care
& my cries he did hear.
Hell he let me lay my head
on his shoulder
& I wanted to be with him forever,
while watching each
other grow older.

My experiences became his
& attributes too.
I was so happy that someone cared
I didn't realize I was his fool.
I was so sucked in,
I didn't care that he started trippin'
My mind, my body & my soul
became his to own.

I was down for whatever
Fellatio, cunnilingus, group sex,
as long as we were together.
Basically, I was his trick
and the only conversations,
were between my mouth
and his dick!

Strung out and impregnated
with his hellacious little imps
I became incoherent,
& started to pimp.
I had brotha's eatin' out my hand
and sistah's fallin too.
We became "family",
known as "his crew"
We were pimpin & trickin'
& we believed all we could fool.

Until this ANGEL
grabbed me by the hand.
"Come here" he said,
"I'm gon' show you a real dance"
for some reason I couldn't resist,
'cause he was fine
and I'm thinkin' to myself
"oh I'm gon' get this"

This way, that way
Umm…that ANGEL broke me down,
sweetly talking in my ear
while the DEVIL
watched with a frown.
Then in one fierce spin
I twirled on my toes
with perfect balance and poise,
my sins went out the door.
When I came to a complete stop,
That DEVIL could no longer watch.

The ANGEL then spread his wings
& I knew I was now free
we hugged and began to laugh
then walked on, hand in hand.

Now do you trust me??
(a conversation with God)

I was shaking, a little scared
and my eyes were swollen.
Exhausted from a meaningless fight
my fears and vulnerability
I had not been controllin'

I was twisted back
with non-existent facts
allowed my self
 to get caught up in a scheme
and it was so deep,
I was even a punk in my dreams.
That is of course when I did sleep;

My body was frail, I was weak
lost my appetite and could not eat.
I let a lie be my truth
not realizing it was my soul
I was going to lose.
See I ignored the gift
that you gave me,
which was to discern
I put everything on me,
forgetting past lessons that I learned.

I gave away my soul eyes
cause I was too busy "getting high"
I began to run in a sprint,
being someone's puppet
and was hell bent.

Until my sprint
became a cross-country run
and the choices I had made,
gave a halt to my fun.
Money and job security
slipped thru my hand,
running from nothing,
I ran and I ran.

I lost my car and had no food
and in the back of my mind
and in my dreams,
I heard the screeching words

"YOU LOSE, YOU LOSE."

I realized
I was in the middle of the wilderness
and that's when I heard
a familiar voice
That said,
"His Greatness"
But you see
I thought I was hearing things,
considering the state of my mind
and being caught up in this scheme.

"Great is thy faithfulness"

It said again,
and I knew without a doubt,
that I wasn't trippin'

"Fast dear child and pray without ceasing I'm going
to remove that Vail and put a stop to you steadily

decreasing."

I placed my hand on my head
because this was something
I did dread.
"But I don't know how to fast
and prayer has left me."

"Obedience dear child,
don't you want to see?
My servant Byron,
he will show you how to fast and pray."

An entire day of talking,
Byron taught me how to fast and pray.
My first day was hard,
I didn't make it half the day.

"Dear child you can do it,
I'm going to give you the strength."

I tried two more times
until the third,
when I was able to go the full length.
Amazingly I was lifted
and a new smile was on my face
I ended my cross-country run,
realizing it was no longer my race.

"J, now you will be able to hear me
and I have given power back to you
but be careful, because Satan knows your weakness,

and he will always try to seduce."

I went back to a place

in which so many did hate.
They didn't know how
to love themselves,
pointing fingers at others,
while putting their sins
on the shelf.

But I thought I was "bad"
because I knew how to fast and pray
I jumped right in
smiling and carryin' on
and indulged in what they had to say.

Before I knew it I was sucked back in,
forgetting past lessons
my mind was going backwards
and doubt so quickly,
started to seep in.
I embraced the enemy foolishly
and was caught up,
right back in my sin.

"I forgive you, I forgive you'
I told them
forgetting what they had done
I ignored character,
the lies they spread
and how they laughed at me out of fun.

I forgot the truth:
THESE PEOPLE DIDN'T LIKE ME

but skippin' about I thought I had clout
and continued to dance
without putting together my two hands.

Again they started to talk
about they way I used to walk
and me thinking I'm so much
indulged in their words,
trying to be tough.
"Yeah I did it, it was me"
I said boldly,
as they were secretly laughing.
Then it hit,
Again, I was at the top of the black list
they put my character
on the back of a moped,
dragging it through the streets.
(be careful she's this be careful she's that to hell
with the facts)

Then I heard that voice again
"J, Great is thy faithfulness"
but what they said
caused tears to pour from my eyes
I was hurt and weakened
because I was tired of the lies.

Again that voice came,
"J, I want you to stand alone,
don't worry about the lies
because just as before,
I will see you through the storm."

I was shaking a little scared

and my eyes were again, swollen.
Exhausted from a meaningless fight,
I finally realized my fears and vulnerability God,
had not been controlling.

"J, I want you to stand alone
and know that I am all that you need.
You've always told the truth,
especially to me,
the lies that they've said is only another way
that allows Satan to seduce.
You see he wants you to give in
and forget, that I have delivered you.
Now I want you to accept your gift:
Discernment, and don't allow Satan to deceive.
Oh yeah, just one other thing,
NOW DO YOU TRUST ME??

Part II
Family Love

Grandpa

Jingling change in your pocket
Magic tricks, allowing us chocolate
Summer trips, teaching us to fish,
Giving us your bed
& the JUKEBOX we all still miss.
Dearest Grandpa,
we're saddened that you are gone.
You were our patriarch
who always stood strong.
In your last years
we remember your tears,
the memories in your eyes
and the love we all shared.
To each of us,
you were warm and someone special
and we were all the same,
"THE GRANDCHILDREN"
of Barney Gambles.
We say thanks Grandpa,
For a kind hand,
the things you've taught us,
and most of all for love
we will miss you
as you now rest
with the Lord above.

Nothin' but LOVE 4 my brothers
(Jacques, Marcel, Anthony, Jason & Damian)

I don't have anything
but love for brothers.

Though distant and far apart
They are all dear to me, and my heart.
From the oldest to the youngest
I consider each of them the best.

Memories, circumstances,
& situations of our past,
has given us a bond through blood
that will always last.

Different views and battles to lose
gives us strength vowing
never to refuse
support, understanding, friendship
and most of all family love.

A tribute 2 my Sisters

(Margot, Jackie, Charron, Shirley, Laurie & Leslie)

In a song of praise
I reminisce about so many days
that each were wonderfully a part
of this crazy world of mine,
I often call ART.
I shout in happiness
that I indeed have true friends
you have been there for me,
even until the end.
My choices, my ways,
and sins of my past days
you've accepted, held my hand
and not once was I rejected.
Silly laughs, sudden mishaps
our growth and true love
that we continue to show.
I salute my sisters
as we continue to grow.
Without ever forgetting one,
with a love so powerful,
absolute and real.
Words on this paper
won't ever measure up
to the love I feel.

LONELY FLOW

Lookin at rain fallin'
sometimes quickly or drippin' slow
I think of my tears
'cause some days they lightly fall
while other days
they are puddles of fear.
I often call them my lonely flow

Do you know what it feels like 2 be motherless?

To yearn for visible love,
acceptance and guidance.
Or have someone to hold you
when life is tough
and set you straight
when you want to give up.
Have conversations about puberty,
sex and a world filled with hate
late night talks of love
and its many faces,
and how one can easily discriminate.

I don't.

Have you ever tried to replace her??
Cause being motherless is damn hard!

After all she was your lifeline
someone to protect you
from all sorts of harm.
Desperately needing a shoulder
'cause you yearn

41

J. Monique Gambles   . . . Just a Season

for Mama's love so much

but you're misunderstood
so you walk the life of a loner
without ever feeling
a motherly touch.

I have.

I think of ways
on many days
of how I could ever ease this pain??
How can I forget a life cut short
because of man's ignorance,
jealousy, deception and distrust??
Some day's I feel like
my heads gon' bust!

It gets hard because I wonder am I lonely or simply
alone.

I just want to lay my head down sometimes on a
soft shoulder and figure out which way do I go?
But I am reminded time & time again
of the absence of true friends
I laugh at there absent faces
those useless vessels
and realize I have only
my lonely flow.

DADDY

Strong, brown, built to last
memories of you and our past.
Strained but filled with love
The bond we shared
was blessed by GOD above.
Deep blue eyes
That didn't dear hide
Hands so strong
In you I never saw wrong.
Your sins and crimes
I needed to be blind.
"cause in me,
you instilled the greatest things.
You told me the world was mine
and I could achieve all that I wanted.
"You can do it" you said
each time I came to you
with eyes filled with tears.
You always knew
how to ease my fears.
Daddy you maybe gone
But your words live on.
And even though some days
I just want to quit.
I hear your words "you can do it"
Rest on Daddy and don't you worry
I'm a big girl now
and I'm going to make it.

Part III
Make's Me want 2 Holla

RedWhiteBlue

Red, white & blue
Well, well, well,
Now tell me,
Why should I give a fuck about You?
Time and time again
You wouldn't let US in
because of the color of our skin.
Nigger this, Nigger that,
NO taxicabs 'cause I'm BLACK!
Poorer schools
Reason why, YOU think we're fools.
And with each social climb
As we tried to find
That great AMERICAN DREAM
(certainly a scheme);
we had to face the truth,
YOU believed
we weren't a part of YOU.
You've never thought we were equal
now things are bad,
so I guess this is the sequel?
A time when things twist
and YOU finally get the gist.
The fact that we are a part of YOU
and all that YOU go through.
So don't be so quick
to push US aside
We're not the ones
with something to hide!
When YOU allowed US to be FREE,
We quickly embraced thee.
We fought in your wars

dying and such

but did YOU truly embrace US?
HELL NO, you said
with eyes filled with disgust!
YOU let others in this country
with the notion they ride for free,
Money for business,
Visas for education
Yet we are your own,
and we aren't gettin' any of this!
Now at this time
When SOME OF THEM
have possibly committed
the worst crime,
YOU ask that we stand together
but what about
when things get better?
Will we truly be equal?
Same crime, same time.
As US
same access?
Standing as true brothers & sisters
and truly getting through this.
Then in the aftermath
We are all on the same path.
When the smoke clears
will YOU finally hear,
we are a part of YOU
and all that YOU go through!

That Great White Lie

You love me; Yeah right
And I'm freed; Nigger psyche!
Dumb founded I sing
Yo' hypocritical anthem,
My—Country-- 'Tis --of --thee...
You have taught me
to read some
No math or science though,
'cause you say I'm dumb.
Truth is, my history reflects
a long line of intellects.
Math, science, astronomy
Language, civilization,
Kings & Queens.
Our land was vast and rich
the worlds best
elements within.
But you've taken that away
bringin' us to this day.
The time of modern day slaves
damn near buried
in our graves.
We are beneath minorities
'cause at least for them,
they are FREE!
Money for education,
money for businesses
but we are
still considered NIGGERS
and we aren't getting SHIT!
Now we can get pimped, prostituted
tricked and deprived

(Dumb ass Niggers; dump liquor & drugs into their

communities they won't survive!)
They'll forget
they come from Kings & Queens
and the fact that civilization
they did bring.
Break down that damn family
And let his DICK
run wild and free.
To hell with the kids,
probably aren't even his!

Use color
to keep them divided,
remember to keep
the darker ones hiding.
From beige to high yellow,
let them dumb mutha fuckas
get one step up from the ghetto.

Now in the matter of education,
internalize in them STAGNATION.
For those damn degrees
will only offer reprieve,

You see ya'll ain't
never been good enough
"cause you don't have the right stuff."
NIGGER,
don't you forget you dumb
you are to forget
where you come from.

Jamaicans, Haitians, West Indians, Africans &
Black Americans too,
HA! I enjoy watching
the fighting between you.
Let the facts that are unclear
become your guns
while you live in fear.

Don't you dare think UNITY
'cause that would
make you all FREE.
Fight vicious and hard
amongst one another
and forget the truth:
You are part of each other!

Do they fear you;
that's right
I am nothing;
Shit, Psyche!

We got's to keep
our heads high
and stop believing,
THAT GREAT WHITE LIE !

HISTORY

They lied 2 me
'cause they said after the civil war, emancipation of
the proclamation,
Yadda, Yadda, Yadda,
I was FREE!!!

Now unless freedom
has taken on new meaning
and consequently,
it represents "shady dealin"
like unjustification,
separation & higher Taxation.
Then they lied,
'cause I ain't FREE!!!

History I tell you,
ain't anything but a lie
It is some distorted notion
that is just a picture of a gray sky
and when looked at, I can only sigh.
It hides the true family tree
'cause pale skin and big lips
is a possible reminder
of what Master did.
So I ignore it as if it never happened.

And let us not forget
O' Mother Africa
who now is nothing but a whore,
diseased, raped, and nothing more.
Just a lifeless vessel,
a political hustle

J. Monique Gambles . . . Just a Season

and a reminder, of what I am not.

History I tell you,
Isn't anything but a lie.
It is a held back tear, hidden fears,
and empty words
that only helps some, survive.

SouthSideBlue

Scattered trash, broken glass
Liquor stores many whom are poor
Shattered dreams, dope feigns
Battles we lose
and empty church pews.
I'm so tired of seeing
south side blues.

Why does the south represent our ignorance?

Worn down streets,
police officers worst beat
abandoned buildings, empty feelings
deprived of so much
'cause no one gives a F***!
Robbed of its beauty,
it becomes wild and unruly.
The south side should be a place
That's alive and blooming.

Why does the south represent underdevelopment?

If we could take a moment
to reflect upon ignored intellect
which WAS immensely great
in our native State(AFRICA)
in which stolen history
does truthfully represent
the South it's riches and betterment.
Yet now it stands pimped
and beat down to no ends.

Why have we become so content?

For it is close to water
the sustainer of life.
To live there,
means one will survive!

So pick up the trash & broken glass
Shut down liquor stores
and help those whom are poor
see your dreams achieved,
thus ridding the community
of dope feigns.
Fix up the streets,
having no need for a "beat"
while our buildings stand tall
and we respectively
represent ourselves
down at City Hall.

And the sustainer of life
will flow through
as it reflects our true beauty
A beautiful blue,
deep strong and free.

ATL(all those lies!)

College degrees,
status and fulfilled dreams
The black man's Mecca,
supposedly a place
where things are better.

In ninety three days
I immediately saw the truth
about this place.
Dressed up black folk
with nice cars & big homes
sorry little Negroes
just worryin' about their own

Cause if you aren't with this clique
or that clique
you aren't gettin' shit!
Black owned politicians thrown
(after I stuff my pockets I'll see what I can loan)

It's like George and Wheezy
movin' on up
except we gon' forget those
who still have it tough
(Hell I bust my ass to make it
& if you think I'm helping you,
your in for a rude awakening')

And that, is the discrepancy
because you have failed to see
by building stronger communities
to help those who are less fortunate
is what will continue
to keep us all FREE!!!

So Negroes please!

ATL, (all those lies.)
The man is still the beneficiary
'cause you still want to compromise
living in your sugar castles
Blowin up cause you think
you on the rise!

Wake up Negroes & walk together
so we can all survive.

Quickness

My patience is quick
My temper even quicker
Steam from my skin
as my rage thickens.
I can't stand depending on people
especially plastic ones
that you see through.
Lyin' mutha fucka's
that r so damn deceitful.
Can I get you to be real?
And my joy you don't steal.
Cause you like extra weight
with drama I don't want to take.
I'm movin' with the quickness
tryin' to stay focused
and handle my business.
My attitude is on
a sistah's got to be strong
and I got two fingers for you
and my motto: "I'm movin' on!"

Judas

Betrayed I lay
a little down on my luck.
Often angry
but then I realize
why should give a fuck?
Cause you turning on me
is like the deal of the day.
It used to get next to me
how one could easily deceive
but when you look at
the character of these
then one has to believe.
It was just a matter of time
that you would try to find
my imperfect ways
and sins of my past days.
As if some justification
to ignore my elevation.
You showed your face of Judas
& I'm actually relieved,
I knew you would do this.
So this here knife in my back
and meaningless words of attack
is actually my motivation
which fuels my determination.

Blackpride/Sexpride

I wish black pride
was as strong as this sex pride
brotha's and sistah's
in deep concentration
lookin' for that next ride.
Imagine if the quest for knowledge was just as great
we wouldn't be lookin' for excuses
for that great escape.
Toe to toe we could stare down
the face of any barrel
discrimination, prejudice, sexism, ridicule and
constant laughter.
Armed with knowledge of our true heritage, history
and legacies
knowing who, what, when how and where ~ there'd
be know mysteries.
But instead we make music, movies, and videos
both braggin'
about who we fucked, sucked,
and how much come we swallowed!
The brain is parallel
to how good a sistah can suck a dick
or she's content because he knows
the difference between
her lips and her clit.
We don't teach our children
about the possibilities of a hard life
we lace them with the finest things
without having a job
and give no explanation
about momma, auntie, grams
and future friends, being dykes!

Chasing a good fuck

they all got played
or been raped
by not even a portion of a man
who has no knowledge of self,
his heritage, history, or legacies
dickin' down anyone,
shit, he's probably gay!
We brag about Fatty pearls,
fatty girls
all night brotha's,
long stroke brotha's
ova cups of cappuccino,
bottles of syrup or primo's and hydro,
high, 'cause somebody
rocked our world!
Reach out and read
a real black history book
(Isis Papers, TheMiseducationoftheNegro)
realizing that for awhile now,
you've been took.
That's right, bamboozled
and run a muck
'cause you wasted so much time,
chasin' a good fuck!
Raise a fist cause time is running out
and you gotta get this.
It's not about the power of the pussy
and how he swings his dick,
it's about knowledge of self,
building strong character,
having respect for yourself
tearing down stereotypes,
ending reckless cycles,

J. Monique Gambles   . . . Just a Season
and fighting for justice!

Part IV
A long walk: war torn Iraq

So what's the deal?
(with the Euphrates)

So, now what's the deal?
I mean does anyone know the appeal
or how you should feel?
I'm talking about history,
the true blood
that runs through you & me
distorted facts, twisted lies
and how we've turned our backs.
I'm talking about ABRAHAM,
ISAAC & JACOB
The twelve tribes, Egypt
and the Bastard Son.
Am I standing alone?
Does anyone care about
where the truth has gone?
I'm standing in tiny grains of sand,
kilometers from Babylon,
UR and Baghdad.
I've crossed the Tigris and gazed down at the
Euphrates,
pissed because of all of the lies
that have been told to me.
'Cause if MOSES did
cross the Red Sea,
leaving Egypt, he kicked it in Saudi??
I'm just searching for facts,
someone said, "The cradle of civilization was in
Iraq."
Which then would mean,
My cousins ADAM & EVE,
Cain, Able, Noah & his crew and Abraham and his

descendants

were Iraqi's??
brothers and sisters
I am in search of the truth
kickin' it in this desert,
I am often aloof.
I see so many shades of brown
and some speckles
that cause me to frown,
realizing that AFRICA is basically invisible on the
map and its countries are called by name with
disregard to where they lie flat.
My mind goes non-stop 'cause I want to know my
true heritage
I'm not talking about slave ships, cotton fields, civil
rights & Dr. King
I'm talking about OUR true history.
Descendants of whom
linked to what?
Great kings of Egypt, Saudi Prince's, Iraqi's or as
NAS say's,
The brothers of KUSH?
Disseminated throughout the land, heterogeneously
beautiful,
I want to know who I am.

Does any one hear me?
'Cause some lies have been told,
check the maps,
research so called facts,
travel and read
and be careful of what
you choose to believe.

I was . . .

Sitting in my backyard
trippin' on some past pleasures
caught up, thinkin' hard,
yet laughing to myself,
because I let down my guard.

Drivin' my Miata
top down with a smile.
The wind played in my curly naps, while my mind,
was the furthest from any mishaps.

In the middle of a huddle,
motioning to my point guards,
yelling at my left hand
& trying to keep #24 and T calm.

Teaching' vocabulary
elaborating on literary terms
turning in lesson plans
and enhancing my post secondary.

Daydreaming about true love
cleaning out my house,
focusing on dreams
and accepting what life
was truly about.

Against war
politics, republicans, hypocrisy
and tax breaks for all those
who had more.

I became part of all that I was against,
a soldier, politician, stingy republican
and a hypocrite!

Invisible War

In a shadow of what was light
I stood in the midst of chaos,
trying to determine,
WHAT WAS RIGHT???

There was a horizon that appeared
to sit beneath infinity.
Awe struck, I began to
search within me.

With continuous blowing sand
there was a mirror image
of a despondent man,
and he's waiting to take part of what has all along
been an invisible war.
To liberate a nation, steal its riches
and nothing more.

I search to understand
my "assumed" role
looking through scripture,
I realize everything
goes back to ones soul.

The ties of your soul
and spiritually where you stand.
The truth of "this matter"
and the true origin of man.

The Journey

We crossed the border
a little past noon.
Sweat and dust, apprehension
anger, confusion and disgust!

I couldn't understand my place
I'm a caregiver, inspirer of all children
a teacher, this had to be
some awful mistake!

The children that emerge
from dirt built huts,
no shoes, chaffed feet, matted hair
caused pain in my guts.

Biting down hard on my lip
still, I did not understand this.
For miles and miles I had to accept,
that I needed to adjust.

A journey in a distant land
learn the truth of an unknowing man.
Breathe in the dust of ancient times
gaze down at secret waters
and so many lifelines.

Spirituality and a walk in faith
speak the language of the eye
fight not Iraqi's,
but, hate filled Americans.

My journey would not be
what they said it would be,
but a walk with an unloving man
who takes, rapes, and dismantles
for the purpose of his elevation

Suffocation would bring me
near to death,
night after night
would feel like my last breath.

The serpent would dance
freely in my dreams
waking up, my tent will echo screams
and exhausted I would fall to my knees.

304, 365, no 425 days later,
I will emerge from my journey
those Iraqi children, with mated hair, no shoes
coming out of dirt built huts
will still smile and wave at me.

I'll never know if it was love, gratitude,
or their need to be free.
I can only whisper a prayer,
thanking God for them
because they prepared me for my journey.

Young, gifted and gone

He played in the schools band
a mother's only son in their household,
he was a man.
A bright smile a warm smile
a kind word a voice heard
he was young, gifted,
yet, he is gone.
In a game of chess
I'm not sure if he was a pawn~
a chance to take
a gamble, or setup.

Because for his life,
someone else gains a stripe,
or rank and prestige,
glorified, while his mama stays on her knees.

In this game of war
he was a pawn, a gamble, and a setup
and a chance so others
could be seen as more.

A short timed lived
a young man that will never be forgotten,
a black man who we will dearly miss
PFC Jonathan Cheatham, we remember you
 as young, gifted & black.

Tradition...

I'm standing on my soap box,
wishin' I had a head full of long locs.
To stand face to face with the man
as sweat beads form at my temple and make
puddles in my hand.
I want to breath fire when I speak,
cut down the ignorance
the stands before me.
Sick and tired, tired and sick
of this so called mutha fucka
whose' breath smells of dick!

Tradition they say
is the glue of this military.
Salute the superior
Less rank equals inferior
Not paid to think
Pushin' so many of us to the brink
Do me, and I'll do you
If you don't kiss ass you're the fool!

What happened to pride and respect?
Hell, leadership that has few regrets.
Decisions that are good
for the soldier
who will day after day,
put on his uniform a bit stronger.
This traditional military
keeps beatin' us down
we're too busy fightin'
this crooked ass system to ever win
a war with Iraq, Liberia,

North Korea or Afghanistan!

I look at my beautiful black brothers
like Thomas, Francis and Adams
their manliness, intellect
and black pride beaming through
their unblemished skin
only to know that time
and time again
they are being robbed by a system
a traditional system,
a crooked ass system,
a good ole boy system
fightin' a war
that they won't ever win.

That leather face, poorly dressed,
no style havin' uncle Sam
with lies in his eyes and a grimace
told us so many times
we could be part of something
that stood for good
we could stop sellin' crack,
dropping out of school
and slummin' it in the hood.
Fight for our country become a man,
have some pride and be treated with respect
be a part of tradition
that same tradition
that never liked the color of our skin,
always treatin' us
like a bounced check!
R.I.P PFC. Adams.

www.ingramcontent.com/pod-product-compliance
Lightning Source LLC
Chambersburg PA
CBHW021822090426
42811CB00032B/1983/J

9780984496020